Table of Contents

CHAPTER ONE

MONEY, MONEY

*Raking and other chores are jobs you could
do for your family or neighbors.*

Imagine you could see into the future. Do you see yourself in a great

job? Are you living in a beautiful home? Do you see yourself wearing nice

clothes and driving a cool car? Right now, it is fun to dream about these

21st Century Skills Library

REAL WORLD MATH: PERSONAL FINANCE

PAYDAY!

Cecilia Minden

Cherry Lake Publishing
Ann Arbor, Michigan

Published in the United States of America by Cherry Lake Publishing
Ann Arbor, MI
www.cherrylakepublishing.com

Math Education Adviser: Timothy J. Whiteford, PhD, Associate Professor of Education, St. Michael's College, Colchester, Vermont

Finance Adviser: Ryan Spaude, CFP®, Kitchenmaster Financial Services, LLC, North Mankato, Minnesota

Library of Congress Cataloging-in-Publication Data
Minden, Cecilia.
 Payday! / by Cecilia Minden.
   p. cm.
 ISBN-13: 978-1-60279-000-1
 ISBN-10: 1-60279-000-0
 1. Finance, Personal—Juvenile literature. 2. Budgets, Personal—Juvenile literature. I. Title.
 HG173.8.M56 2008
 332.024—dc22   2007003878

*Cherry Lake Publishing would like to acknowledge the work of
The Partnership for 21st Century Skills.
Please visit* www.21stcenturyskills.org *for more information.*

things. But when you grow up, you will have to pay for your house, car, and clothes. That means getting a job.

Do you get an allowance? Many kids have to do chores for the money they receive. Children's allowances often increase as they grow up and can do more. Jack, age five, gets $2.00 a week. He can do simple tasks. He might set the table or help put away groceries. Serena, age nine, receives $6.00 a week. She can do more difficult tasks. She might vacuum, clean, or cook simple meals. The allowances Jack and Serena receive are related to the chores they can do.

Adults are also paid according to what they do. Some jobs pay by the hour. A job requiring few skills gets a low hourly rate. A job requiring more skills gets paid at a higher rate. Some people are paid a **salary**. A salary is a set amount of money a worker earns in a year. Salaried jobs generally

require more education. These jobs usually come with **benefits**. Benefits are extra things such as health insurance and life insurance that the **employer** pays for. Sometimes, an employer pays the entire cost of a benefit. Other times, the employer splits the cost with the **employee**. Some employers also put money into their employees' retirement accounts.

You may need to attend a vocational school to become an auto mechanic.

The career you choose is one factor that determines your income. One big difference between high- and low-paying jobs is the level of education needed to do the job. Colleges and universities prepare students for many different jobs. Some of the careers that require a college education include lawyer, scientist, and teacher. Some people learn a specific skill at a **vocational** school. For example, they might study auto repair. Other people advance in their careers through on-the-job training. Some jobs do not require a high school diploma. These jobs often pay very little and usually do not include benefits. These low-paying jobs include janitor and

21st Century Content

Generally, the more education you have, the more you will get paid. Being an electrician does not require a college degree, but it does require a lot of on-the-job training. The average salary for an electrician is $31,500 a year. By comparison, a person with a two-year engineering technology degree working in the electronics field may earn $57,000 a year. An electronics engineer with a four-year degree can earn more than $100,000 a year.

Do you have a great jump shot? Are you planning on making it rich in sports? Is this a good plan for your future? Think about it. There are 360 professional basketball players in the National Basketball Association (NBA). But every year, more than half a million American boys play high school basketball. So what are their chances of making it to the NBA? Practically zero!

Even if you're the very best high school player in your state, you still need a backup plan!

store clerk. In most jobs, as your experience and responsibilities increase, your salary will go up, too.

Can't wait to get that first big paycheck? There are a few things you need to know about how much money you will take home.

The amount of money you earn depends on the job you are doing.

CHAPTER TWO

Where'd My Money Go?

You landed that dream job. Now it's payday! If you take your annual salary and divide by 12, you get your **gross monthly pay**. But don't expect the entire gross monthly pay to end up in your bank account.

When you get an allowance, it is yours to keep. Your parents may put some restrictions on it. For instance, you may have to put some in a savings account. The rest you can spend on whatever you want.

Unlike an allowance, a paycheck comes with automatic **deductions**. Deductions are amounts subtracted from paychecks before the worker gets the money. Federal, state, and local taxes are deductions. Deductions

nings Information	Current
nal Gross	4,389.30
ctions	0.00
tions	0.00
rtime	0.00
EARNINGS TOTAL	4,389.3
	351.1
-Taxable Gross	3,971.
able Gross	

atutory & Other Deductions	C
eral Withholding	
itional Federal Withholding	
te Withholding	
itional State Withholding	
DI	
icare	
icare Buyout	
te Disability Insurance	
S	
S	
nate Retirement	

Your paycheck stub will list the amounts deducted from your paycheck for things such as income taxes and insurance.

also include payments for health insurance. Health insurance pays for medical expenses and sometimes for dental and vision care.

Everyone pays **Social Security tax** and **Medicare tax**. This money is put in reserve until you retire or become disabled. Some people also have deductions for money that is put into a retirement account. Some companies allow you to have donations to charities, such as United Way, taken directly from your paycheck.

It's exciting to get your first paycheck. You can pay all your bills and still have money left over. You can spend it on whatever you want. Do you want some new shoes? Tickets to the baseball game would be great.

REAL WORLD MATH CHALLENGE

Marco just got his first monthly paycheck. His gross monthly pay is $2,000. Listed below are his deductions. **How much money does he have left to deposit in his bank account?**

Deductions

Federal Income Tax	$140.19
Social Security and Medicare Tax	$136.02
State Income Tax	$78.27
City Income Tax	$9.96
Health Insurance	$33.06
Retirement Account	$75.00
United Way	$25.00

(Turn to page 29 for the answer)

Spending most of your money at the beginning of the month will leave you with very little, if any, money at the end of the month. What happens if you need gas for your car, but you won't get paid for five more days? Where did the money go? Some of it was used to pay bills, but what happened to the rest of it? How do you make sure this doesn't happen again? Let's find out!

CHAPTER THREE

DO THE MATH: FIND YOUR INCOME AND EXPENSES

You need a budget to make sure you spend your money wisely and make

it last all month. A budget is a plan for how you will spend your money.

Having a plan will help you make better choices. Only you can make a

budget for yourself. Only you know what you have to have and what you

It is smart to sit down and make a plan for how
you will spend the money you earn.

can do without. To create a budget, you need to know your income and your expenses.

What is your income? Do you get an allowance in exchange for chores you do around the house? This is income you receive on a regular basis.

What are your expenses? Expenses are the things you spend money on. People like to spend money on

REAL WORLD MATH CHALLENGE

Dara is saving for a new skateboard. The board she wants costs $50.00. She receives $6.00 a week for her allowance. Last week, she bought a magazine ($1.95), a candy bar ($0.60), and some hair clips ($0.95). She put the rest in the bank to save for the skateboard.

If Dara puts the same amount in the bank each week, how long will it take for her to get her skateboard?

How long will it take if she also saves the $25.00 her grandma gave her for her birthday?

(Turn to page 29 for the answers)

Different people spend their money in different ways.

different things. In a family, one child may rarely spend money. Another

child may have trouble hanging on to money for even a day. Before you

can make a budget, you need to make a list of where your money is going.

One way to do this is to get a small notepad. Make sure it fits in your pocket so you always have it with you. Every time you buy something, write down the item and the amount. No purchase is too small. Be sure you include every single thing you buy. Do this for two weeks. It will give you some good ideas about how you are spending your money. After two weeks, look to see where your money went. Surprised? Maybe there is a way to get more for your money.

Make a list of categories: Food, Entertainment, Transportation, Savings, Charity, and Other. Put every item that you spent money on in one of these categories. Some items may fit in a couple of categories. You decide which category best fits the purchase.

Now what do you do with this list?

CHAPTER FOUR

DO THE MATH: CREATE A BUDGET

Ask your parents about computer programs that they use that might help you manage your money.

Y ou've made a list of everything you've bought in the last two weeks. Now you need to take a look at how you spent your money. Is one column much longer than the others? Maybe the "Other" list is the longest. That is

Learning & Innovation Skills

It is hard to make decisions about the best ways to spend your money. It involves asking yourself thoughtful questions and making choices. A good way to start is to think about what you actually need. A need fulfills a goal. If you are thirsty, you can get a drink from a water fountain. That will satisfy the need. If you bought a super-size soda instead, that is because you wanted the soda. You don't need a soda. Both water and soda will quench your thirst, but one is free and the other costs money. If a water fountain isn't around, you still have choices in what you buy. You could buy a small soda that will quench your thirst at half the cost. To make good decisions about your budget, you have to be honest about whether you really need something or only want it.

where you spent the most money. But what do you have to show for it? Look at each item on that list. Did you *need* to buy it, or did you just *want* it?

To save up for more expensive items, you need to cut down on what you spend now. Think about items on the list that you wanted but didn't need. Are you glad you bought them? Would you be just as happy if you hadn't? To make a budget, you have to decide what's important to you.

When creating a budget, think about big purchases you want to make. That pair of

Buying a new pair of jeans may require that
you make a short-term savings plan.

jeans you want costs $30.00, but your allowance is only $10.00 a week.

You're going to have to put aside some money every week if you want to

buy the jeans. This is a short-term goal. And what about your class trip to

Washington, D.C., in the spring? Your parents say you need to pay for half

the expenses. That's a long-term goal.

Sometimes, you need extra money quickly but your allowance for the week is gone. If you borrow ahead on next week's allowance, then you won't have any money later. The best way to handle emergencies is to plan ahead. When you are making your budget, set aside some money for emergencies. Add to your emergency fund each week so that when something unexpected comes up, you have the money to pay for it.

So now you've decided which expenses are important and how much to spend on them. You've thought about your long- and short-term goals. You want to put money away for emergencies and give money to charity. Now you're ready to write down your budget.

Say your weekly allowance is $6.00. Write that at the top of the page. Then write down how much you're going to spend on expenses. Let's say that amount is $3.50. You may want to divide this into different categories, like food or entertainment. In addition, you're

putting away $1.50 for a video game you've just got

to have. The emergency fund will get $0.50, and

$0.50 goes into the charity fund. You've done it!

You've created a budget.

Making a budget is personal. Your parents and friends can give you advice, but you must make the final decision about how to divide up your money. There is no single right answer. They might have very different ideas about what is important and what isn't. It is good to listen to those ideas, because they may help you figure out what you want to do. But in the end, you will have to decide on the right budget for you.

Buying food for your family is an expense that your parents have to plan for when they make a budget.

REAL WORLD MATH CHALLENGE

Angelina's allowance is $7.00 a week. She also receives $5.00 a week for helping a neighbor with child care.

Every month, she gives money to an animal shelter. She is saving money for a trip her family is taking next summer to Hawaii. She also wants to go to a concert next month with her friends. Her friend Kim wants to go shopping tomorrow. So many places to spend her money!

It's time to set up a budget. She decides to donate 10 percent of her income to charity. She will save 15 percent for long-term goals and 25 percent for short-term goals. The remaining 50 percent is spending money.

What is Angelina's weekly income? How much does she set aside for charity? How much for long-term goals? How much for short-term goals? How much does Angelina have to spend shopping with Kim?

(Turn to page 29 for the answers)

You now have a budget and you are trying to stick to it. It is hard to do! You'd like to have a little more money to work with. What can you do?

Let's find out!

CHAPTER FIVE

GETTING AHEAD

Offering to do extra chores for pay is one way to increase your income.

Sometimes your allowance will not pay for what you want. You don't want to wipe out all of your savings, either. What can you do?

One possibility is to increase your income. You can do this by offering to do extra chores. Walk around the house and yard with a notepad. Make a list of things you see that need to be done. Which jobs can you do to bring in some extra cash?

Think first about the chores you normally do for your allowance. If your job is putting away the laundry, maybe you could also wash, dry, and fold the laundry. If your job is taking out the trash, maybe you could empty all the wastebaskets, sort the recyclable material, and sweep out the garage. Once you've thought of some extra jobs, try to figure out what you think is a fair payment for each job.

Choose a time when your parents are not busy doing something else. Sit down with them and explain that you would like to earn some extra money. Give your parents the list of jobs and prices. Ask them if there is something on the list that they would like to hire you to do. Then **negotiate** a price that you all think is fair.

You may also decide that your current allowance isn't enough. How do you negotiate a higher amount? First, make a list of your expenses.

REAL WORLD MATH CHALLENGE

Katie is saving up for a new mountain bike. She has saved $226.89. She needs another $72.00. Her parents agree to pay her to do extra chores on the weekend. They will give her $4.00 an hour for doing the laundry and washing the car or $6.00 an hour for raking leaves while also keeping an eye on her little sister.

She works two hours every Saturday.

How long will it take her to earn the money for the bike doing the laundry and washing the car?

How long will it take her if she agrees to babysit and do yard work?

(Turn to page 29 for the answers)

Then write down the reasons you think you should get more money. Your parents might be more open to a higher amount if they see that you really need the money. Ask your parents if you can set a time to talk with them. Don't try to talk about money when they are busy cooking, cleaning, or driving. You will want their full attention.

Keep in mind that when you negotiate, both sides usually have to give a little. Your parents might agree to give you a higher allowance, but it

If you like to do yard work, mowing lawns for neighbors may be a good way to earn money.

might not be as much as you wanted. And remember, if you accept more money, you will probably have to do more chores.

You can also make more money by doing jobs for other people in the neighborhood. Look at the list of chores you made for your parents. Could you do these same jobs for your neighbors? Write up a flyer with your name, the jobs you will do, and prices. Then distribute the flyer to your neighbors. Remember, the best advertising is word of mouth. If you do a good job for one neighbor, that person will recommend you to another neighbor.

There are other ways to save money and stretch your budget that do not require extra work. But they do take a little time. Say there's a hat you saw at the mall that costs $7.50. Your allowance is $8.00 a week, so you could buy it. But if you do that, you won't have money to spend on anything else. Instead, plan on saving $2.50 a week until you can buy the hat. Taking the time to save will also give you time to shop around. If you spend a little more time, you'll be sure you know exactly which hat you want. You might also find a discount store that is selling the same hat for less money. Or you might find a store that is offering a coupon. If you find

Clipping coupons is one way to save money when shopping for groceries and other items.

a coupon that gives you 20 percent off any item you buy at the store, you will be able to get the $7.50 hat for only $6.00. Taking the time to shop around can help you save!

You work hard for your money. By planning ahead, using a budget, and shopping carefully, you'll get much more for your money.

REAL WORLD MATH CHALLENGE ANSWERS

Chapter Two

Page 12

The total of the deductions is $497.50.

$140.19 + $136.02 + $78.27 + $9.96 + $33.06 + $75.00 + $25.00 = $497.50

Marco's paycheck will be $1,502.50.

$2,000 − $497.50 = $1,502.50

Chapter Three

Page 14

Dara spent $3.50.

$1.95 + $0.60 + $0.95 = $3.50

Dara saves $2.50 each week.

$6.00 − $3.50 = $2.50

If she uses only money from her allowance, it will take Dara 20 weeks to save enough money for her skateboard.

$50.00 ÷ $2.50 = 20

After saving her grandma's gift, Dara still needs $25.00. It will take her 10 weeks to save that much from her allowance.

$50.00 − $25.00 = $25.00

$25.00 ÷ $2.50 = 10

Chapter Four

Page 22

Angelina's income is $12.00 per week.

$7.00 + $5.00 = $12.00

Angelina will give $1.20 to charity, save $1.80 for long-term goals, and save $3.00 for short-term goals. She has $6.00 to spend shopping with Kim.

10% of $12.00 = .10 x 12.00 = $1.20

15% of $12.00 = .15 x 12.00 = $1.80

25% of $12.00 = .25 x 12.00 = $3.00

50% of $12.00 = .50 x 12.00 = $6.00

Chapter Five

Page 25

Katie would earn $8.00 a week doing the laundry and washing the car. She would earn $12.00 a week babysitting her sister and raking leaves.

2 x $4.00 = $8.00

2 x $6.00 = $12.00

It would take Katie 9 weeks to earn the money for the bike doing laundry and washing the car. If she babysits her sister and rakes leaves, it will take her only 6 weeks.

$72.00 ÷ $8.00 = 9

$72.00 ÷ $12.00 = 6

GLOSSARY

benefits (BEH-nuh-fits) extra things such as health insurance and life insurance that an employer pays for

deductions (dih-DUK-shunz) money subtracted from a paycheck for taxes and benefits

employee (im-ploi-YEE) one who does a job for someone else

employer (im-PLOI-yur) one who hires others to do a job

gross monthly pay (GROWSS MUNTH-lee PAY) income before deductions

Medicare tax (MEH-dih-kayr TAKS) a tax used to pay for a government-funded health insurance program

minimum (MIH-nuh-mum) the least amount possible

negotiate (neh-GO-shee-ate) to discuss with others ways to reach an agreement

salary (SAH-luh-ree) a fixed amount of money a worker is paid for services

Social Security tax (SO-shul sih-KYUR-uh-tee TAKS) a tax used to pay for a government-funded retirement program

vocational (vo-KAY-shuh-nul) related to training in a specific trade

For More Information

Books

Godfrey, Neale S. Neale S. *Godfrey's Ultimate Kids' Money Book.*
New York: Simon and Schuster Books for Young Readers, 1998.

Schwartz, Stuart, and Craig Conley. *Budgeting Your
Money.* Mankato, MN: Capstone, 1999.

Web Sites

Young Investor: Earn It
www.younginvestor.com/kids/earnIt/
Includes information, puzzles, and games about earning money

Social Studies for Kids—Want vs. Need: Basic Economics
www.socialstudiesforkids.com/articles/economics/wantsandneeds1.htm
For information on how to tell the difference between
something you want and something you need

INDEX

ABOUT THE AUTHOR

Cecilia Minden, PhD, is a literacy consultant and the author of many books for children. She is the former director of the Language and Literacy Program at Harvard Graduate School of Education in Cambridge, Massachusetts. She would like to thank fifth-grade math teacher Beth Rottinghaus for her help with the Real World Math Challenge problems. Cecilia lives with her family in North Carolina.